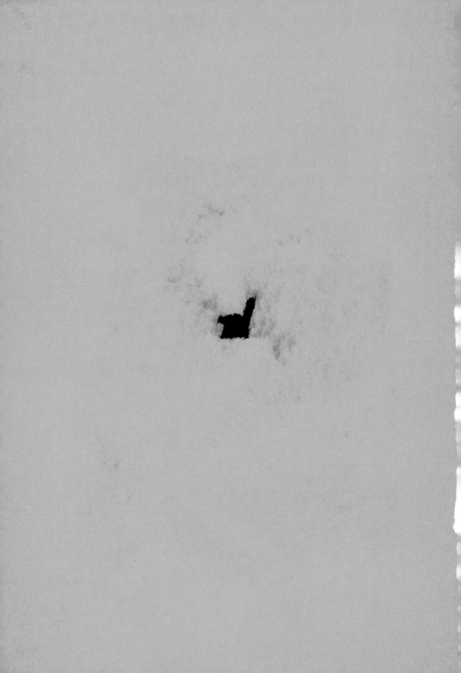

A GIFT FOR

_____

FROM

_____

THIS IS
LOVE

The Extraordinary Story of Jesus

MAX LUCADO

THOMAS NELSON
Since 1798

NASHVILLE   DALLAS   MEXICO CITY   RIO DE JANEIRO

THIS IS LOVE

Published in Nashville, Tennessee, by Thomas Nelson. Thomas Nelson' is a registered trademark of Thomas Nelson, Inc.

Thomas Nelson, Inc. titles may be purchased in bulk for educational, business, fund-raising, or sales promotional use. For information, please e-mail SpecialMarkets@ThomasNelson.com.

Scripture references are from the following sources: The NEW KING JAMES VERSION (NKJV) ©1979, 1980, 1982, 1992, 2002 Thomas Nelson, Inc., Publisher. The Holy Bible, *New International Version®, NIV®.* Copyright © 1973, 1978, 1984 by Biblica, Inc.™ Used by permission of Zondervan. All rights reserved worldwide. *The Message* (MSG), copyright © 1993, 1994, 1995, 1996, 2000, 2001, 2002. Used by permission of NavPress Publishing Group. *New American Standard Bible* (NASB), © 1960, 1962, 1963, 1968, 1971, 1972, 1973, 1975, 1977, 1995 by the Lockman Foundation. Used by permission. The *New Century Version®* (NCV). Copyright © 2005 by Thomas Nelson, Inc. Used by permission. All rights reserved. The *Amplified Bible* (AMP). The Amplified New Testament, copyright © 1954, 1958, 1987 by the Lockman Foundation. *The Living Bible* (TLB), copyright © 1971 by Tyndale House Publishers, Wheaton, Illinois 60187. All rights reserved. The *Contemporary English Version* (CEV) © 1995 by the American Bible Society. All rights reserved. The *Revised Standard Version* of the Bible (RSV), copyright © 1946, 1952, 1971 by the Division of Christian Education of the National Council of the Churches of Christ in the USA.

Compiled by Terri Gibbs
Editorial Supervision: Karen Hill, Executive Editor for Max Lucado
Development Editor: Lisa Stilwell
Design: Koechel Peterson & Associates, Inc., Minneapolis, MN

Photographs unless otherwise noted are from photos.com
        pages 4-5 Flickr.com | Fort Photo; pages 26-27 Flickr.com | aycee_2000 (Alan Carmichael)

ISBN 978-1-4003-2006-6
ISBN 978-1-4041-7510-5
This book is a portion of the previously published *His Name Is Jesus*, ISBN: 978-14041-418-6736

www.thomasnelson.com

Printed and bound in China

CONTENTS

JESUS WAS, AT ONCE, COMMON AND NOT; alternately normal and heroic. One minute blending in with the domino players in the park, the next commanding the hell out of madmen, disease out of the dying, and death out of the dead. Who was this man who spoke as easily with kids and fishermen as widows and waves? It is the question that has echoed down through the centuries to us today.

HIS STORY WAS EXTRAORDINARY. He called himself divine, yet allowed a minimum-wage Roman soldier to drive a nail into his wrist. He demanded purity, yet stood for the rights of a repentant whore. He called men to march, yet refused to allow them to call him King. He sent men into all the world, yet equipped them with only bended knees and memories of a resurrected carpenter.

WE CAN'T REGARD HIM AS SIMPLY A GOOD TEACHER. His claims are too outrageous to limit him to the company of Socrates or Aristotle. Nor can we categorize him as one of many prophets sent to reveal eternal truths. His own claims eliminate that possibility.

WHO IS HE? My prayer is that as you read this book Jesus will emerge from a wavy figure walking out of a desert mirage to become the touchable face of a best friend. My idea is simple. Let's look at some places he went and some people he touched. Join me on a quest for his "God-manness." You may be amazed.

More important, you may be changed.

MAX LUCADO

He stilled a storm with one command.

He raised the dead with one proclamation.

He rerouted the history of the world with one life.

HIS DEATH

Jesus...

The palm that held the universe
took the nail of a soldier.

It encircled the angels and starstruck the shepherds
in the Bethlehem pasture.

Jesus radiates it.

John beheld it.

Peter witnessed it on Transfiguration Hill.

Christ will return enthroned in it.

Heaven will be illuminated by it.

One glimpse, one taste, one sampling,
and your faith will never be the same . . .

Glory.

God's glory.

Every act of heaven reveals God's glory. Every act of
Jesus did the same.

IT'S NOT ABOUT ME

GLORY! *Glory*

Mercy IS THE DEEPEST GESTURE *of kindness.*

The evening meal was being served, and the devil had already prompted Judas Iscariot, son of Simon, to betray Jesus. Jesus knew that the Father had put all things under his power, and that he had come from God and was returning to God; so he got up from the meal, took off his outer clothing, . . . and began to wash his disciples' feet, drying them with the towel that was wrapped around him.

JOHN 13:2–5 NIV

JESUS WASHES HIS DISCIPLES' FEET

IT HAS BEEN A LONG DAY. Jerusalem is packed with Passover guests, most of whom clamor for a glimpse of the Teacher. The spring sun is warm. The streets are dry. And the disciples are a long way from home. A splash of cool water would be refreshing.

The disciples enter [the room], one by one, and take their places around the table. On the wall hangs a towel, and on the floor sits a pitcher and a basin. Any one of the disciples could volunteer for the job, but not one does.

After a few moments, Jesus stands and removes his outer garment. He wraps a servant's girdle around his waist, takes up the basin, and kneels before one of the disciples. He unlaces a sandal and gently lifts the foot and places it in the basin, covers it with water, and begins to bathe it. One by one, one grimy foot after another, Jesus works his way down the row.

In Jesus' day the washing of feet was a task reserved not just for servants, but for the lowest of servants. . . . The servant at the bottom of the totem pole was expected to be the one on his knees with the towel and basin.

In this case the One with the towel and basin is the King of the universe. Hands that shaped the stars now wash away filth. Fingers that formed mountains now massage toes. And the One before whom all nations will one day kneel now kneels before his disciples. Hours before his own death, Jesus' concern is singular. He wants his disciples to know how much he loves them. . . .

You can be sure Jesus knows the future of these feet he is washing. These twenty-four feet will not spend the next day following their Master, defending his cause. These feet will dash for cover at the flash of a Roman sword. Only one pair of feet won't abandon him in the garden. . . . Judas won't even make it that far! He will abandon Jesus that very night at the table. . . .

What a passionate moment when Jesus silently lifts the feet of his betrayer and washes them in the basin.

Jesus knows what these men are about to do. He knows they are about to perform the vilest act of their lives. By morning they will bury their heads in shame and look down at their feet in disgust. And when they do, he wants them to remember how his knees knelt before them and he washed their feet. . . .

He forgave their sin before they even committed it. He offered mercy before they even sought it.

Just Like Jesus

Content to be known as a carpenter.

HAPPY TO BE MISTAKEN FOR THE GARDENER.

HE SERVED HIS FOLLOWERS BY WASHING THEIR FEET.

HE SERVES US BY DOING THE SAME.

Each morning he gifts us with beauty.

Each Sunday he calls us to his table.

Each moment he dwells in our hearts.

A LOVE WORTH GIVING

GOD WAS NEVER MORE SOVEREIGN

than in the details

of the death of his Son.

The Sufferings of His Broken Heart

GO WITH ME FOR A MOMENT to witness what was perhaps the foggiest night in history. The scene is very simple; you'll recognize it quickly. A grove of twisted olive trees. Ground cluttered with large rocks. A low stone fence. A dark, dark night.

Now, look into the picture. Look closely through the shadowy foliage. See that person? See that solitary figure? What's he doing? Flat on the ground. Face stained with dirt and tears. Fists pounding the hard earth. Eyes wide with a stupor of fear. Hair matted with salty sweat. Is that blood on his forehead?

That's Jesus. Jesus in the Garden of Gethsemane.

Maybe you've seen the classic portrait of Christ in the garden. Kneeling beside a big rock. Snow-white robe. Hands peacefully folded in prayer. A look of serenity on his face. Halo over his head. A spotlight from heaven illuminating his golden-brown hair.

Now, I'm no artist, but I can tell you one thing. The man who painted that picture didn't use the Gospel of Mark as a pattern. When Mark wrote about that painful night, he used phrases like these: "Horror and dismay came over him," "My heart is ready to break with grief," and "He went a little forward and threw himself on the ground."

Does this look like the picture of a saintly Jesus resting in the palm of God? Hardly. Mark used black paint to describe this scene. We see an agonizing, straining, and struggling Jesus. We see a "man of sorrows" (Isaiah 53:3 NASB). We see a man struggling with fear, wrestling with commitments, and yearning for relief.

We see Jesus in the fog of a broken heart.

The writer of Hebrews would later pen, "During the days of Jesus' life on earth, he offered up prayers and petitions with loud cries and tears to the one who could save him from death" (Hebrews 5:7 NIV).

My, what a portrait! Jesus is in pain. Jesus is on the stage of fear. Jesus is cloaked, not in sainthood, but in humanity.

The next time the fog finds you, you might do well to remember Jesus in the garden. The next time you think that no one understands, reread the fourteenth chapter of Mark. The next time your self-pity convinces you that no one cares, pay a visit to Gethsemane. And the next time you wonder if God really perceives the pain that prevails on this dusty planet, listen to him pleading among the twisted trees.

The next time you are called to suffer, pay attention. It may be the closest you'll ever get to God. Watch closely. It could very well be that the hand that extends itself to lead you out of the fog is a pierced one.

JESUS BETRAYED BY JUDAS

WHEN BETRAYAL COMES, what do you do? Get out? Get angry? Get even? You have to deal with it some way. Let's see how Jesus dealt with it.

Begin by noticing how Jesus saw Judas. "Jesus answered, 'Friend, do what you came to do'" (Matthew 26:50 NCV).

Of all the names I would have chosen for Judas, it would not have been "friend." What Judas did to Jesus was grossly unfair. There is no indication that Jesus ever mistreated Judas. There is no clue that Judas was ever left out or neglected. When, during the Last Supper, Jesus told the disciples that his betrayer sat at the table, they didn't turn to one another and whisper, "It's Judas. Jesus told us he would do this."

They didn't whisper it because Jesus never said it. He had known it. He had known what Judas would do, but he treated the betrayer as if he were faithful.

It's even more unfair when you consider the betrayal was Judas' idea. The religious leaders didn't seek him; Judas sought them. "What will you pay me for giving Jesus to you?" he asked (Matthew 26:15 NCV). The betrayal would have been more palatable had Judas been propositioned by the leaders, but he wasn't. He propositioned them.

And Judas' method . . . again, why did it have to be a kiss? (Matthew 26:48–49).

And why did he have to call him "Teacher"? (Matthew 26:49). That's a title of respect. The incongruity of his words, deeds, and actions—I wouldn't have called Judas "friend."

But that is exactly what Jesus called him.

Why? Jesus could see something we can't. . . .

Jesus knew Judas had been seduced by a powerful foe. He was aware of the wiles of Satan's whispers (he had just heard them himself). He knew how hard it was for Judas to do what was right.

He didn't justify what Judas did. He didn't minimize the deed. Nor did he release Judas from his choice. But he did look eye to eye with his betrayer and try to understand.

As long as you hate your enemy, a jail door is closed and a prisoner is taken. But when you try to understand and release your foe from your hatred, then the prisoner is released and that prisoner is you.

AND THE ANGELS WERE SILENT

John tells us that "Judas came there with a group of soldiers and some guards from the leading priests and Pharisees" (JOHN 18:3 NCV). . . . ❋ I always had the impression that a handful of soldiers arrested Jesus. I was wrong. At minimum two hundred soldiers were dispatched to deal with a single carpenter and his eleven friends! ❋ Also present were "some guards." This was the temple police. They were assigned to guard the holiest place during the busiest time of the year. They must have been among Israel's finest. ❋ And then there was Judas. One of the inner circle. Not only had Satan recruited the Romans and the Jews, he had infiltrated the cabinet. Hell must have been rejoicing. There was no way Jesus could escape. Satan sealed every exit. His lieutenants anticipated every move, except one. ❋ Jesus had no desire to run. He had no intent of escape. He hadn't come to the garden to retreat. What they found among the trees was no coward; what they found was a conqueror.

A Gentle Thunder

ON THE EVE OF THE CROSS,

Jesus made his decision.

HE WOULD RATHER

go to hell for you

THAN GO TO HEAVEN WITHOUT YOU

PETER DENIES KNOWING JESUS

Peter had bragged, "Everyone else may stumble . . .
but I will not" (Matthew 26:33 NCV). Yet he did. . . .

He stood and stepped out of hiding and followed the noise till he
saw the torch-lit jury in the courtyard of Caiaphas.

He stopped near a fire and warmed his hands. . . . Other people
near the fire recognized him. "You were with him," they challenged.
"You were with the Nazarene." Three times people said it, and each
time Peter denied it. And each time Jesus heard it.

Please understand that the main character in this drama of denial
is not Peter, but Jesus. Jesus, who knows the hearts of all people,
knew the denial of his friend. Three times the salt of Peter's
betrayal stung the wounds of the Messiah.

How do I know Jesus knew? Because of what he did. Then "the
Lord turned and looked straight at Peter" (Luke 22:61 NIV).
When the rooster crowed, Jesus turned. His eyes searched for
Peter and they found him. At that moment there were no soldiers,
no accusers, no priests. At that predawn moment in Jerusalem
there were only two people—Jesus and Peter.

Peter would never forget that look.

On Trial before Pilate

The most famous trial in history is about to begin.

Jesus

THE JUDGE IS SHORT and patrician with darting eyes and expensive clothes. His graying hair trimmed and face beardless. He is apprehensive, nervous about being thrust into a decision he can't avoid. Two soldiers lead him down the stone stairs of the fortress into the broad courtyard. Shafts of morning sunlight stretch across the stone floor.

As he enters, Syrian soldiers dressed in short togas yank themselves and their spears erect and stare straight ahead. The floor on which they stand is a mosaic of broad, brown, smooth rocks. On the floor are carved the games the soldiers play while awaiting the sentencing of the prisoner.

But in the presence of the procurator, they don't play.

A regal chair is placed on a landing five steps up from the floor. The magistrate ascends and takes his seat. The accused is brought into the room and placed below him. A covey of robed religious leaders follow, walk over to one side of the room, and stand.

Pilate looks at the lone figure. . . .

"Are you the king of the Jews?"

For the first time, Jesus lifts his eyes. He doesn't raise his head, but he lifts his eyes. He peers at the procurator from beneath his brow. Pilate is surprised at the tone in Jesus' voice.

"Those are your words."

Before Pilate can respond, the knot of Jewish leaders mock the accused from the side of the courtroom.

"See, he has no respect."

"He stirs the people!"

"He claims to be king!"

Pilate doesn't hear them. "Those are your words." No defense. No explanation. No panic. The Galilean is looking at the floor again.

Something about this country rabbi appeals to Pilate. He's different from the bleeding hearts who cluster outside. He's not like the leaders with the chest-length beards who one minute boast of a sovereign God and the next beg for lower taxes. His eyes are not the fiery ones of the zealots who are such a pain to the *Pax Romana* he tries to keep. He's different, this upcountry Messiah. . . .

Pilate wants to let Jesus go. *Just give me a reason,* he thinks, almost aloud. *I'll set you free.*

His thoughts are interrupted by a tap on the shoulder. A messenger leans and whispers. Strange. Pilate's wife has sent word not to get involved in the case. Something about a dream she had.

Pilate walks back to his chair, sits, and stares at Jesus. "Even the gods are on your side?" he states with no explanation.

He has sat in this chair before. It's a curule seat: cobalt blue with thick, ornate legs. The traditional seat of decision. By sitting on it Pilate transforms any room or street into a courtroom. It is from here he renders decisions.

How many times has he sat here? How many stories has he heard? How many pleas has he received? How many wide eyes have stared at him, pleading for mercy, begging for acquittal?

But the eyes of this Nazarene are calm, silent. They don't scream. They don't dart. Pilate searches them for anxiety . . . for anger. He doesn't find it. What he finds makes him shift again.

He's not angry with me. He's not afraid . . . he seems to understand.

Pilate is correct in his observation. Jesus is not afraid. He is not angry. He is not on the verge of panic. For he is not surprised. Jesus knows his hour and the hour has come.

Pilate is correct in his curiosity. Where, if Jesus is a leader, are his followers? What, if he is the Messiah, does he intend to do? Why, if he is a teacher, are the religious leaders so angry at him?

Pilate is also correct in his question. "What should I do with Jesus, the one called the Christ?" (Matthew 27:22 NCV).

Perhaps you, like Pilate, are curious about this one called Jesus. You, like Pilate, are puzzled by his claims and stirred by his passions. . . .

What do you do with a man who calls himself the Savior, yet condemns systems? What do you do with a man who knows the place and time of his death, yet goes there anyway?

Pilate's question is yours. "What will I do with this man, Jesus?"

You have two choices.

You can reject him. That is an option. You can, as have many, decide that the idea of God's becoming a carpenter is too bizarre—and walk away.

Or you can accept him. You can journey with him. You can listen for his voice amid the hundreds of voices and follow him.

AND THE ANGELS WERE SILENT

Christ lived the life we could not live

AND TOOK THE PUNISHMENT WE COULD NOT TAKE

to offer the hope we cannot resist.

WHY?

Jesus was angry enough to purge the temple,

> hungry enough to eat raw grain,
>
> distraught enough to weep in public,
>
> fun loving enough to be called a drunkard,
>
> winsome enough to attract kids,
>
> weary enough to sleep in a storm-bounced boat,
>
> poor enough to sleep on dirt and borrow a coin for a sermon illustration,
>
> radical enough to get kicked out of town,
>
> responsible enough to care for his mother,
>
> tempted enough to know the smell of Satan,
>
> and fearful enough to sweat blood.

WHY? Why would heaven's finest Son endure earth's toughest pain? So you would know that "he is able . . . to run to the cry of . . . those who are being tempted and tested and tried" (Hebrews 2:18 AMP).

Whatever you are facing, he knows how you feel.

NEXT DOOR SAVIOR

He, who can dig the Grand Canyon

WITH HIS PINKIE,

THINKS YOU'RE WORTH

his death on Roman timber.

The Soldiers Wanted Jesus' Blood

The soldiers? *They wanted blood.*

So they scourged Jesus. The legionnaire's whip consisted of leather straps with lead balls on each end. His goal was singular: Beat the accused within an inch of his death and then stop. Thirty-nine lashes were allowed but seldom needed. A centurion monitored the prisoner's status. No doubt Jesus was near death when his hands were untied and he slumped to the ground.

The whipping was the first deed of the soldiers.

The crucifixion was the third. (No, I didn't skip the second. We'll get to that in a moment.) Though his back was ribboned with wounds, the soldiers loaded the crossbeam on Jesus' shoulders and marched him to the Place of the Skull and executed him.

We don't fault the soldiers for these two actions. After all, they were just following orders. But what's hard to understand is what they did in between. Here is Matthew's description:

"Jesus was beaten with whips and handed over to the soldiers to be crucified. The governor's soldiers took Jesus into the governor's palace, and they all gathered around him. They took off his clothes and put a red robe on him. Using thorny branches, they made a crown, put it on his head, and put a stick in his right hand. Then the soldiers bowed before Jesus and made fun of him, saying, 'Hail, King of the Jews!' They spat on Jesus. Then they took his stick and began to beat him on the head. After they finished, the soldiers took off the robe and put his own clothes on him again. Then they led him away to be crucified" (Matthew 27:26–31 NCV).

The soldiers' assignment was simple: Take the Nazarene to the hill and kill him. But they had another idea. They wanted to have some fun first. Strong, rested, armed soldiers encircled an exhausted, nearly dead, Galilean carpenter and beat up on him. The scourging was commanded. The crucifixion was ordered. But who would draw pleasure out of spitting on a half-dead man?

Spitting isn't intended to hurt the body—it can't. Spitting is intended to degrade the soul, and it does. What were the soldiers doing? Were they not elevating themselves at the expense of another? They felt big by making Christ look small.

Allow the spit of the soldiers to symbolize the filth in our hearts. And then observe what Jesus does with our filth. He carries it to the cross.

Through the prophet he said, "I did not hide my face from mocking and spitting" (Isaiah 50:6 NIV). Mingled with his blood and sweat was the essence of our sin.

God could have deemed otherwise. In God's plan, Jesus was offered wine for his throat, so why not a towel for his face? Simon carried the cross of Jesus, but he didn't mop the cheek of Jesus. Angels were a prayer away. Couldn't they have taken the spittle away?

They could have, but Jesus never commanded them to. For some reason, the One who chose the nails also chose the saliva. Along with the spear and the sponge of man, he bore the spit of man.

The sinless One took on the face of a sinner so that we sinners could take on the face of a saint.

He Chose the Nails.

THE CROWN OF THORNS

AN UNNAMED SOLDIER took branches—mature enough to bear thorns, nimble enough to bend—and wove them into a crown of mockery, a crown of thorns.

Throughout Scripture thorns symbolize, not sin, but the consequence of sin. Remember Eden? After Adam and Eve sinned, God cursed the land: "So I will put a curse on the ground. . . . The ground will produce thorns and weeds for you, and you will eat the plants of the field" (Genesis 3:17–18 NCV). Brambles on the earth are the product of sin in the heart.

The fruit of sin is thorns—spiny, prickly, cutting thorns.

I emphasize the "point" of the thorns to suggest a point you may have never considered: If the fruit of sin is thorns, isn't the thorny crown on Christ's brow a picture of the fruit of our sin that pierced his heart?

What is the fruit of sin? Step into the briar patch of humanity and feel a few thistles. Shame. Fear. Disgrace. Discouragement. Anxiety. Haven't our hearts been caught in these brambles?

The heart of Jesus, however, had not. He had never been cut by the thorns of sin. What you and I face daily, he never knew. Anxiety? He never worried! Guilt? He was never guilty! Fear? He never left the presence of God! Jesus never knew the fruit of sin . . . until he became sin for us.

He Chose the Nails

Simon from Cyrene Carries Jesus' Cross

SIMON GRUMBLES under his breath. His patience is as scarce as space on the Jerusalem streets. He'd hoped for a peaceful Passover. The city is anything but quiet. Simon prefers his open fields. And now, to top it off, the Roman guards are clearing the path for some who-knows-which dignitary who'll march his soldiers and strut his stallion past the people.

"There he is!"

Simon's head and dozens of others turn. In an instant they know. This is no dignitary.

"It's a crucifixion," he hears someone whisper. Four soldiers. One criminal. Four spears. One cross. The inside corner of the cross saddles the convict's shoulders. Its base drags in the dirt. Its top teeters in the air. The condemned man steadies the cross the best he can but stumbles beneath its weight. He pushes himself to his feet and lurches forward before falling again. Simon can't see the man's face, only a head wreathed with thorny branches.

A sour-faced centurion grows more agitated with each diminishing step. He curses the criminal and the crowd.

"Hurry up!"

"Little hope of that," Simon says to himself.

The cross-bearer stops in front of Simon and heaves for air. Simon winces at what he sees. The beam rubbing against an already-raw back. Rivulets of crimson streaking the man's face. His mouth hangs open, both out of pain and out of breath.

"His name is Jesus," someone speaks softly. "Move on!" commands the executioner.

But Jesus can't. His body leans and feet try, but he can't move. The beam begins to sway. Jesus tries to steady it, but can't. Like a just-cut tree, the cross begins to topple toward the crowd. Everyone steps back, except the farmer. Simon instinctively extends his strong hands and catches the cross.

Jesus falls face-first in the dirt and stays there. Simon pushes the cross back on its side. The centurion looks at the exhausted Christ and the bulky bystander and needs only an instant to make the decision. He presses the flat of his spear on Simon's shoulder.

"You! Take the cross!"

Simon dares to object. "Sir, I don't even know the man!"

"I don't care. Take up the cross!"

Simon growls, steps out of the crowd onto the street, and balances the timber against his shoulder, out of anonymity into history, and becomes the first in a line of millions who will take up the cross and follow Christ.

He did literally what God calls us to do figuratively: Take up the cross and follow Jesus. "If any of you want to be my followers, you must forget about yourself. You must take up your cross each day and follow me" (Luke 9:23 CEV).

THE CROSS.

Strange that a tool of torture would

COME TO EMBODY A MOVEMENT OF HOPE.

THE SIGN ON CHRIST'S CROSS

"This is the King of the Jews."

A hand-painted, Roman-commissioned sign. . . .

Why is a sign placed over the head of Jesus?

Why are the words written in three languages?

Could it be that this piece of wood is a picture of God's devotion? A symbol of his passion to tell the world about his Son? . . .

Pilate had intended the sign to threaten and mock the Jews. But God had another purpose . . . Pilate was God's instrument for spreading the gospel.

Every passerby could read the sign, for every passerby could read Hebrew, Latin, or Greek—the three great languages of the ancient world. "Hebrew was the language of Israel, the language of religion; Latin the language of the Romans, the language of law and government; and Greek the language of Greece, the language of culture. Christ was declared king in them all" (McHugh and McHugh, *The Trial of Jesus*). God had a message for each. "Christ is king." The message was the same, but the languages were different. Since Jesus was a king for all people, the message would be in the tongues of all people.

HE CHOSE THE NAILS

Two Thieves, Two Crosses

SKULL'S HILL—windswept and stony. The thief—gaunt and pale. . . .

His situation is pitiful. He's taking the last step down the spiral staircase of failure. One crime after another. One rejection after another. Lower and lower he descended until he reached the bottom—a crossbeam and three spikes.

He can't hide who he is. His only clothing is the cloak of his disgrace. No fancy jargon. No impressive résumé. No Sunday school awards. Just a naked history of failure.

He sees Jesus. . . .

He hears the jests and the insults and sees the man remain quiet. He sees the fresh blood on Jesus' cheeks, the crown of thorns scraping Jesus' scalp, and he hears the hoarse whisper, "Father, forgive them."

Why do they want him dead?

Slowly the thief's curiosity offsets the pain in his body. He momentarily forgets the nails rubbing against the raw bones of his wrists and the cramps in his calves.

He begins to feel a peculiar warmth in his heart: He begins to care; he begins to care about this peaceful martyr.

There's no anger in his eyes, only tears.

He looks at the huddle of soldiers throwing dice in the dirt, gambling for a ragged robe. He sees the sign above Jesus' head. It's painted with sarcasm: King of the Jews. . . .

All of a sudden, his thoughts are exploded by the accusations of the criminal on the other cross. He, too, has been studying Jesus, but studying through the blurred lens of cynicism.

> *"So you're the Messiah, are you? Prove it by saving yourself—*
> *and us, too, while you're at it!"* (Luke 23:39 TLB).

It's an inexplicable dilemma—how two people can hear the same words and see the same Savior, and one see hope and the other see nothing but himself.

It was all the first criminal could take. Perhaps the crook who hurled the barb expected the other crook to take the cue and hurl a few of his own. But he didn't. No second verse was sung. What the bitter-tongued criminal did hear were words of defense.

> *"Don't you fear God?"*

When it seems that everyone has turned away, a crook places himself between Jesus and the accusers and speaks on his behalf.

> *"Don't you even fear God when you are dying? We deserve to die*
> *for our evil deeds, but this man hasn't done one thing wrong"*
> (Luke 23:40 TLB).

The soldiers look up. The priests cease chattering. Mary wipes her tears and raises her eyes. No one had even noticed the fellow, but now everyone looks at him.

Perhaps even Jesus looks at him. Perhaps he turns to see the one who had spoken when all others had remained silent. Perhaps he fights to focus his eyes on the one who offered this final gesture of love he'd receive while alive. I wonder, did he smile as this sheep straggled into the fold?

For that, in effect, is exactly what the criminal is doing. He is stumbling to safety just as the gate is closing. Lodged in the thief's statement are the two facts that anyone needs to recognize in order to come to Jesus. Look at the phrase again. Do you see them?

"We are getting what we deserve. This man has done nothing wrong"
(Luke 23:41 NIV).

We are guilty and he is innocent.

We are filthy and he is pure.

We are wrong and he is right.

He is not on that cross for his sins. He is there for ours.

And once the crook understands this, his request seems only natural. As he looks into the eyes of his last hope, he makes the same request any Christian has made.

"Remember me when you come into your kingdom"
(Luke 23:42 NIV).

No stained-glass homilies. No excuses. Just a desperate plea for help.

At this point Jesus performs the greatest miracle of the cross. Greater than the earthquake. Greater than the tearing of the temple curtain. Greater than the darkness. Greater than the resurrected saints appearing on the streets.

He performs the miracle of forgiveness. A sin-soaked criminal is received by a blood-stained Savior.

"Today you will be with me in Paradise. This is a solemn promise"
(Luke 23:43 TLB).

WHEN ASKED TO DESCRIBE

the width of his love,

Christ stretched one hand to the right
and the other to the left and had them nailed
in that position

so you would know HE DIED LOVING YOU.

He died loving you.

THE TALE OF THE CRUCIFIED CROOK

If anyone was ever worthless, this one was. If any man ever deserved dying, this man probably did. If any fellow was ever a loser, this fellow was at the top of the list.

Perhaps that is why Jesus chose him to show us what he thinks of the human race.

Maybe this criminal had heard the Messiah speak. Maybe he had seen him love the lowly. Maybe he had watched him dine with the punks, pickpockets, and potmouths on the streets. Or maybe not.

Maybe the only thing he knew about this Messiah was what he now saw: a beaten, slashed, nail-suspended preacher. His face crimson with blood, his bones peeking through torn flesh, his lungs gasping for air.

Something, though, told him he had never been in better company. And somehow he realized that even though all he had was prayer, he had finally met the One to whom he should pray.

No Wonder They Call Him the Savior

Nails didn't hold God to a cross.

Love did.

"Father, Forgive Them"

The dialogue that Friday morning was bitter.

From the onlookers, "Come down from the cross if you are the Son of God!"

From the religious leaders, "He saved others but he can't save himself."

From the soldiers, "If you are the king of the Jews, save yourself."

Bitter words. Acidic with sarcasm. Hateful. Irreverent. Wasn't it enough that he was being crucified? Wasn't it enough that he was being shamed as a criminal? Were the nails insufficient? Was the crown of thorns too soft? Had the flogging been too short?

For some, apparently so. . . .

Of all the scenes around the cross, this one angers me the most. What kind of people, I ask myself, would mock a dying man? Who would be so base as to pour the salt of scorn upon open wounds? How low and perverted to sneer at one who is laced with pain. . . .

The words thrown that day were meant to wound. And there is nothing more painful than words meant to hurt. . . .

If you have suffered or are suffering because of someone else's words, you'll be glad to know that there is a balm for this laceration. Meditate on these words from 1 Peter 2:23 (NIV):

"When they hurled their insults at him, he did not retaliate; when he suffered, he made no threats. Instead, he entrusted himself to him who judges justly."

Did you see what Jesus did not do? He did not retaliate. He did not bite back. He did not say, "I'll get you!" "Come on up here and say that to my face!" "Just wait until after the resurrection, buddy!" No, these statements were not found on Christ's lips.

Did you see what Jesus did do? He "entrusted himself to him who judges justly." Or said more simply, he left the judging to God. He did not take on the task of seeking revenge. He demanded no apology. He hired no bounty hunters and sent out no posse. He, to the astounding contrary, spoke on their defense. "Father, forgive them, for they do not know what they are doing" (Luke 23:34 NIV). . . .

"THEY DON'T KNOW WHAT THEY ARE DOING."

And when you think about it, they didn't. They hadn't the faintest idea what they were doing. They were a stir-crazy mob, mad at something they couldn't see, so they took it out on, of all people, God. But they didn't know what they were doing.

Yes, the dialogue that Friday morning was bitter. The verbal stones were meant to sting. How Jesus, with a body wracked with pain, eyes blinded by his own blood, and lungs yearning for air, could speak on behalf of some heartless thugs is beyond my comprehension. Never, never have I seen such love. If ever a person deserved a shot at revenge, Jesus did. But he didn't take it. Instead he died for them. How could he do it? I don't know. But I do know that all of a sudden my wounds seem very painless. My grudges and hard feelings are suddenly childish.

Sometimes I wonder if we don't see Christ's love as much in the people he tolerated as in the pain he endured.

Amazing Grace.

No Wonder They Call Him the Savior

The cross.

Can you turn any direction without seeing one? Perched atop a chapel. Carved into a graveyard headstone. Engraved in a ring or suspended on a chain. The cross is the universal symbol of Christianity. An odd choice, don't you think? Strange that a tool of torture would come to embody a movement of hope. The symbols of other faiths are more upbeat: the six-pointed star of David, the crescent moon of Islam, a lotus blossom for Buddhism. Yet a cross for Christianity? An instrument of execution? ❊ Why is the cross the symbol of our faith? To find the answer look no farther than the cross itself. Its design couldn't be simpler. One beam horizontal—the other vertical. One reaches out—like God's love. The other reaches up—as does God's holiness. One represents the width of his love; the other reflects the height of his holiness. The cross is the intersection. The cross is where God forgave his children without lowering his standards. ❊ How could he do this? In a sentence: God put our sin on his Son and punished it there. ❊ "God put the wrong on him who never did anything wrong, so we could be put right with God" (2 Corinthians 5:21 MSG).

HE CHOSE THE NAILS

JESUS SPENT OVER THREE DECADES

WADING THROUGH THE MUCK

AND MIRE OF OUR SIN

YET STILL SAW ENOUGH BEAUTY IN US

TO DIE FOR OUR MISTAKES.

JESUS ASKS JOHN TO CARE FOR HIS MOTHER

Mary is older now. The hair at her temples is gray. Wrinkles have replaced her youthful skin. Her hands are calloused. She has raised a houseful of children. And now she beholds the crucifixion of her firstborn.

One wonders what memories she conjures up as she witnesses his torture. The long ride to Bethlehem, perhaps. A baby's bed made from cow's hay. Fugitives in Egypt. At home in Nazareth. Panic in Jerusalem. "I thought he was with you!" Carpentry lessons. Dinner table laughter.

And then the morning Jesus came in from the shop early, his eyes firmer, his voice more direct. He had heard the news. "John is preaching in the desert." Her son took off his nail apron, dusted off his hands, and with one last look said good-bye to his mother. They both knew it would never be the same again. In that last look they shared a secret, the full extent of which was too painful to say aloud.

Mary learned that day the heartache that comes from saying good-bye. From then on she was to love her son from a distance: on the edge of the crowd, outside of a packed house, on the shore of the sea. . . .

"Woman, behold your son!"

John fastened his arm around Mary a little tighter. Jesus was asking him to be the son that a mother needs and that in some ways he never was.

Jesus looked at Mary. His ache was from a pain far greater than that of the nails and thorns. In their silent glance they again shared a secret. And he said good-bye.

NO WONDER THEY CALL HIM THE SAVIOR

Jesus

Thirsty on the Cross

Jesus' final act on earth was intended to win your trust.

Later, knowing that all was now completed, and so that the Scripture would be fulfilled, Jesus said, "I am thirsty." A jar of wine vinegar was there, so they soaked a sponge in it, put the sponge on a stalk of the hyssop plant, and lifted it to Jesus' lips. When he had received the drink, Jesus said, "It is finished." With that, he bowed his head and gave up his spirit.

JOHN 19:28–30 NIV

THIS IS THE FINAL ACT of Jesus' life. In the concluding measure of his earthly composition, we hear the sounds of a thirsty man.

And through his thirst—through a sponge and a jar of cheap wine—he leaves a final appeal.

"You can trust me."

Jesus. Lips cracked and mouth of cotton. Throat so dry he couldn't swallow, and voice so hoarse he could scarcely speak. He is thirsty. To find the last time moisture touched these lips you need to rewind a dozen hours to the meal in the Upper Room. Since tasting that cup of wine, Jesus has been beaten, spat upon, bruised, and cut. He has been a cross-carrier and sin-bearer, and no liquid has salved his throat. He is thirsty.

Why doesn't he do something about it? Couldn't he? Did he not cause jugs of water to be jugs of wine? Did he not make a wall out of the Jordan River and two walls out of the Red Sea? Didn't he, with one word, banish the rain and calm the waves? Doesn't Scripture say that he "turned the desert into pools" (Psalm 107:35 NIV) and "the hard rock into springs" (Psalm 114:8 NIV)?

Did God not say, "I will pour water on him who is thirsty" (Isaiah 44:3 NKJV)?

If so, why does Jesus endure thirst?

While we are asking this question, add a few more. Why did he grow weary in Samaria (John 4:6), disturbed in Nazareth (Mark 6:6), and angry in the temple (John 2:15)? Why was he sleepy in the boat on the Sea of Galilee (Mark 4:38), sad at the tomb of Lazarus (John 11:35), and hungry in the wilderness (Matthew 4:2)?

Why? And why did he grow thirsty on the cross?

He didn't have to suffer thirst. At least, not to the level he did. Six hours earlier he'd been offered drink, but he refused it.

"They brought Jesus to the place called Golgotha (which means The Place of the Skull). Then they offered him wine mixed with myrrh, but *he did not take it.* And they crucified him. Dividing up his clothes, they cast lots to see what each would get" (Mark 15:22–24 NIV, italics mine).

Before the nail was pounded, a drink was offered. Mark says the wine was mixed with myrrh. Matthew described it as wine mixed with gall. Both myrrh and gall contain sedative properties that numb the senses. But Jesus refused them. He refused to be stupefied by the drugs, opting instead to feel the full force of his suffering.

Why? Why did he endure all these feelings? Because he knew you would feel them too.

He knew you would be weary, disturbed, and angry. He knew you'd be sleepy, grief-stricken, and hungry. He knew you'd face pain. If not the pain of the body, the pain of the soul . . . pain too sharp for any drug. He knew you'd face thirst. If not a thirst for water, at least a thirst for truth, and the truth we glean from the image of a thirsty Christ is—he understands.

And because he understands, we can come to him.

The hill is quiet now. Not still but quiet. For the first time all day there is no noise. The clamor began to subside when the darkness—that puzzling midday darkness—fell. Like water douses a fire, the shadows doused the ridicule. No more taunts. No more jokes. No more jesting. And, in time, no more mockers. One by one the onlookers turned and began the descent.

That is, all the onlookers except you and me. We did not leave. We came to learn. And so we lingered in the semidarkness and listened. We listened to the soldiers cursing, the passersby questioning, and the women weeping. But most of all, we listened to the trio of dying men groaning. Hoarse, guttural, thirsty groans. They groaned with each rolling of the head and each pivot of the legs.

But as the minutes became hours, these groans diminished. The three seemed dead. Were it not for the belabored breathing, you would have thought they were.

Then he screamed. As if someone had yanked his hair, the back of his head slammed against the sign that bore his name, and he screamed. Like a dagger cuts the curtain, his scream cut the dark. Standing as straight as the nails would permit, he cried as one calling for a lost friend, "Eloi!"

His voice was raspy, scratchy. Reflections of the torch flame danced in his wide eyes. "My God!"

Ignoring the volcano of erupting pain, he pushed upward until his shoulders were higher than his nailed hands. "Why have you forsaken me?"

The soldiers stared. The weeping of the women ceased. One of the Pharisees sneered sarcastically, "He's calling Elijah."

No one laughed.

He'd shouted a question to the heavens, and you half expected heaven to shout one in return.

And apparently it did. For the face of Jesus softened, and an afternoon dawn broke as he spoke a final time. "It is finished. Father, into your hands I commit my spirit."

As he gave his final breath, the earth gave a sudden stir. A rock rolled, and a soldier stumbled. Then, as suddenly as the silence was broken, the silence returned.

And now all is quiet. The mocking has ceased. There is no one to mock.

The soldiers are busy with the business of cleaning up the dead. Two men have come. Dressed well and meaning well, they are given the body of Jesus.

He Chose the Nails

55

A Cry of Victory

"IT IS FINISHED."

Stop and listen. Can you imagine the cry from the cross? The sky is dark. The other two victims are moaning. The jeering mouths are silent. Perhaps there is thunder. Perhaps there is weeping. Perhaps there is silence. Then Jesus draws in a deep breath, pushes his feet down on that Roman nail, and cries, "It is finished!"

What was finished?

The history-long plan of redeeming man was finished. The message of God to man was finished. The works done by Jesus as a man on earth were finished. The task of selecting and training ambassadors was finished. The job was finished. The song had been sung. The blood had been poured. The sacrifice had been made. The sting of death had been removed. It was over.

A cry of defeat? Hardly. Had his hands not been fastened down I dare say that a triumphant fist would have punched the dark sky. No, this is no cry of despair. It is a cry of completion. A cry of victory. A cry of fulfillment. Yes, even a cry of relief.

It's over.

An angel sighs. A star wipes away a tear.

"TAKE ME HOME."

> Yes, take him home.
> Take this prince to his king.
> Take this son to his father.
> Take this pilgrim to his home.
> (He deserves a rest.)

"TAKE ME HOME."

> Come ten thousand angels!
> Come and take this wounded troubadour to
> the cradle of his Father's arms!

Farewell manger's infant.
Bless you holy ambassador.
Go Home death slayer.
Rest well sweet soldier.

The battle is over.

No Wonder They Call Him the Savior

It is finished?

How could Jesus say he was finished?
There were still the hungry to feed, the sick to heal,
the untaught to instruct, and the unloved to love.
How could he say he was finished?
Simple. He had completed his designated task.
His commission was fulfilled.
The painter could set aside his brush,
the sculptor lay down his chisel, the writer put away his pen.
The job was done.

JUST LIKE JESUS

Do you feel a need for affirmation?

You need only pause at the base of the cross
and be reminded of this:

*The maker of the stars
would rather die for you
than live without you.*

And that is a fact.

Jesus

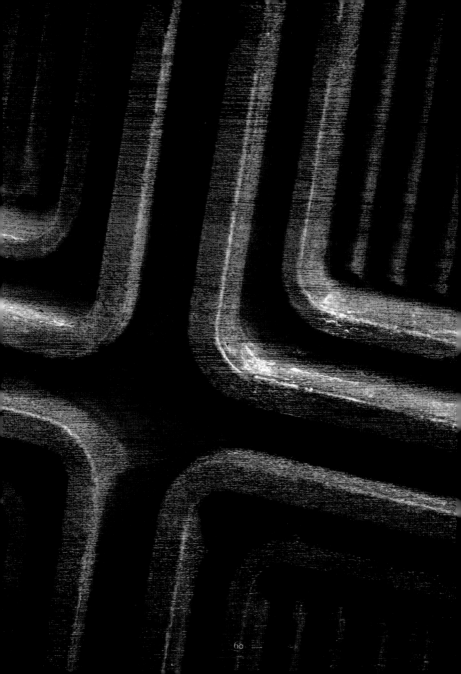

The Centurion at the Foot of the Cross

The centurion was no stranger to finality. Over the years he'd grown callous to the screams of the crucified. He'd mastered the art of numbing his heart. But this crucifixion plagued him.

THE DAY BEGAN as had a hundred others—dreadfully. It was bad enough to be in Judea, but it was hell to spend hot afternoons on a rocky hill supervising the death of pickpockets and rabble-rousers. Half the crowd taunted, half cried. The soldiers griped. The priests bossed. It was a thankless job in a strange land. He was ready for the day to be over before it began.

He was curious at the attention given to the flat-footed peasant. He smiled as he read the sign that would go on the cross. The condemned looked like anything but a king. His face was lumpy and bruised. His back arched slightly and his eyes faced downward. "Some harmless hick," mused the centurion. "What could he have done?"

Then Jesus raised his head. He wasn't angry. He wasn't uneasy. His eyes were strangely calm as they stared from behind the bloody mask. He looked at those who knew him—moving deliberately from face to face as if he had a word for each.

For just a moment he looked at the centurion—for a second the Roman looked into the purest eyes he'd ever seen. He didn't know what the look meant. But the look made him swallow and his stomach feel empty. As he watched the soldier grab the Nazarene and yank him to the ground, something told him this was not going to be a normal day.

As the hours wore on, the centurion found himself looking more and more at the one on the center cross. He didn't know what to do with the Nazarene's silence. He didn't know what to do with his kindness.

But most of all, he was perplexed by the darkness. He didn't know what to do with the black sky in midafternoon. No one could explain it. . . . No one even tried. One minute the sun, the next the darkness. One minute the heat, the next a chilly breeze. Even the priests were silenced.

For a long while the centurion sat on a rock and stared at the three silhouetted figures. Their heads were limp, occasionally rolling from side to side. The jeering was silent . . . eerily silent. Those who had wept, now waited.

Suddenly the center head ceased to bob. It yanked itself erect. Its eyes opened in a flash of white. A roar sliced the silence. "It is finished" (John 19:30 NIV). It wasn't a yell. It wasn't a scream. It was a roar . . . a lion's roar. From what world that roar came the centurion didn't know, but he knew it wasn't this one.

The centurion stood up from the rock and took a few paces toward the Nazarene. As he got closer, he could tell that Jesus was staring into the sky. There was something in his eyes that the soldier had to see. But after only a few steps, he fell. He stood and fell again. The ground was shaking, gently at first and now violently. He tried once more to walk and was able to take a few steps and then fall . . . at the foot of the cross.

He looked up into the face of this one near death. The King looked down at the crusty old centurion. Jesus' hands were fastened; they couldn't reach out. His feet were nailed to timber; they couldn't walk toward him. His head was heavy with pain; he could scarcely move it. But his eyes . . . they were afire.

They were unquenchable. They were the eyes of God.

Perhaps that is what made the centurion say what he said. He saw the eyes of God. He saw the same eyes that had been seen by a near-naked adulteress in Jerusalem, a friendless divorcée in Samaria, and a four-day-dead Lazarus in a cemetery. The same eyes that didn't close upon seeing man's futility, didn't turn away at man's failure, and didn't wince upon witnessing man's death.

"It's all right," God's eyes said. "I've seen the storms and it's still all right."

The centurion's convictions began to flow together like rivers. "This was no carpenter," he spoke under his breath. "This was no peasant. This was no normal man."

He stood and looked around at the rocks that had fallen and the sky that had blackened. He turned and stared at the soldiers as they stared at Jesus with frozen faces. He turned and watched as the eyes of Jesus lifted and looked toward home. He listened as the parched lips parted and the swollen tongue spoke for the last time.

"Father, into your hands I commit my spirit" (Luke 23:46 NIV).

Had the centurion not said it, the soldiers would have. Had the centurion not said it, the rocks would have—as would have the angels, the stars, even the demons. But he did say it. It fell to a nameless foreigner to state what they all knew.

"Surely he was the Son of God" (Matthew 27:54 NIV).

SIX HOURS ONE FRIDAY

IT WAS NOT THE SOLDIERS WHO KILLED HIM,

NOR THE SCREAMS OF THE MOB:

It was his devotion to us.

Six hours, one Friday.

To the casual observer the six hours are mundane. A shepherd with his sheep, a housewife with her thoughts, a doctor with his patients. But to the handful of awestruck witnesses, the most maddening of miracles is occurring.

God is on a cross. The creator of the universe is being executed.

Spit and blood are caked to his cheeks, and his lips are cracked and swollen. Thorns rip his scalp. His lungs scream with pain. His legs knot with cramps. Taut nerves threaten to snap as pain twangs her morbid melody. . . . And there is no one to save him, for he is sacrificing himself.

It is no normal six hours . . .
it is no normal Friday.

SIX HOURS ONE FRIDAY

HIS
RESURRECTION

Jesus...

the moment he
removed the stone,
he removed all reason
for doubt.

CHRIST'S RESURRECTION

is an exploding flare

announcing to all sincere seekers

that it is

SAFE TO BELIEVE.

Later, Joseph from Arimathea asked Pilate if he could take the body of Jesus.
(Joseph was a secret follower of Jesus, because he was afraid of the Jews.)
Pilate gave his permission, so Joseph came and took Jesus' body away.
Nicodemus, who earlier had come to Jesus at night, went with Joseph. He
brought about seventy-five pounds of myrrh and aloes. These two men took
Jesus' body and wrapped it with the spices in pieces of linen cloth, which is how
the Jewish people bury the dead. In the place where Jesus was crucified, there
was a garden. In the garden was a new tomb that had never been used before.

JOHN 19:38–41 NCV

RELUCTANT DURING CHRIST'S LIFE but courageous at his death, Joseph and Nicodemus came to serve Jesus. They came to bury him. They ascended the hill bearing the burial clothing.

Pilate had given his permission.

Joseph of Arimathea had given a tomb.

Nicodemus had brought the spices and linens.

John states that Nicodemus brought seventy-five pounds of myrrh and aloes. The amount is worth noting, for such a quantity of burial ointments was typically used only for kings.

He Chose the Nails

THE SEAL ON THE TOMB

To protect a letter, you seal the envelope. To keep air out of a jar, you seal its mouth with a rubber-ringed lid. To keep oxygen from the wine, you seal the opening with cork and wax. To seal a deal, you might sign a contract or notarize a signature. Sealing declares ownership and secures contents.

The most famous New Testament "sealing" occurred with the tomb of Jesus. Roman soldiers rolled a rock over the entrance and "set a seal on the stone" (Matthew 27:66 NASB). Archaeologists envision two ribbons stretched in front of the entrance, glued together with hardened wax that bore the imprimatur of the Roman government—SPQR *(Senatus Populusque Romanus)*—as if to say, "Stay away! The contents of this tomb belong to Rome."

Their seal, of course, proved futile.

COME THIRSTY

JESUS' BURIAL

WHEN PILATE LEARNED that Jesus was dead, he asked the soldier if they were certain. They were. Had they seen the Nazarene twitch, had they heard even one moan, they would have broken his legs to speed his end. But there was no need. The thrust of a spear removed all doubt. The Romans knew their job. And their job was finished. They pried loose the nails, lowered his body, and gave it to Joseph and Nicodemus.

Joseph of Arimathea. Nicodemus the Pharisee. They sat in seats of power and bore positions of influence. Men of means and men of clout. But they would've traded it all for one breath out of the body of Jesus. He had answered the prayer of their hearts, the prayer for the Messiah. As much as the soldiers wanted him dead, even more these men wanted him alive.

As they sponged the blood from his beard, don't you know they listened for his breath? As they wrapped the cloth around his hands, don't you know they hoped for a pulse? Don't you know they searched for life?

But they didn't find it.

So they do with him what they were expected to do with a dead man. They wrap his body in clean linen and place it in a tomb. Joseph's tomb. Roman guards are stationed to guard the corpse. And a Roman seal is set on the rock of the tomb. For three days, no one gets close to the grave.

But then, Sunday arrives. And with Sunday comes light—a light within the tomb. A bright light? A soft light? Flashing? Hovering? We don't know. But there was a light. For he is the light. And with the light came life. Just as the darkness was banished, now the decay is reversed. Heaven blows and Jesus breathes. His chest expands. Waxy lips open. Wooden fingers lift. Heart valves swish and hinged joints bend.

And, as we envision the moment, we stand in awe.

We stand in awe not just because of what we see, but because of what we know. . . . "We know that when Jesus was raised from the dead it was a signal of the end of death-as-the-end. Never again will death have the last word. When Jesus died, he took sin down with him, but alive he brings God down to us" (Romans 6:5–7 MSG).

WHEN CHRIST COMES

BUT THEN, SUNDAY ARRIVES.

Jesus

GOD LIVES TO HEAR YOUR HEARTBEAT.

He loves to hear your prayers.

HE'D DIE FOR YOUR SIN

BEFORE HE'D LET YOU DIE IN YOUR SIN,

so he did.

COULD THERE HAVE BEEN a greater tragedy for John than a dead Jesus? Three years earlier John had turned his back on his career and cast his lot with this Nazarene carpenter. Earlier in the week John had enjoyed a ticker-tape parade as Jesus and the disciples entered Jerusalem. Oh, how quickly things had turned! The people who had called him king on Sunday called for his death the following Friday. These linens were a tangible reminder that his friend and his future were wrapped in cloth and sealed behind a rock.

John didn't know on that Friday what you and I now know. He didn't know that Friday's tragedy would be Sunday's triumph. John would later confess that he "did not yet understand from the Scriptures that Jesus must rise from the dead" (John 20:9 NCV).

THAT'S WHY WHAT HE DID ON SATURDAY IS SO IMPORTANT.

We don't know anything about this day; we have no passage to read, no knowledge to share. All we know is this: When Sunday came, John was still present. When Mary Magdalene came looking for him, she found him.

Jesus was dead. The Master's body was lifeless. John's friend and future were buried. But John had not left. Why? Was he waiting for the resurrection? No. As far as he knew, the lips were forever silent and the hands forever still. He wasn't expecting a Sunday surprise. Then why was he here?

You'd think he would have left. Who was to say that the men who crucified Christ wouldn't come after him? The crowds were pleased with one crucifixion; the religious leaders might have called for more. Why didn't John get out of town?

Perhaps the answer was pragmatic; perhaps he was taking care of Jesus' mother.

Or perhaps he didn't have anywhere else to go. Could be he didn't have any money or energy or direction . . . or all of the above.

Or maybe he lingered because he loved Jesus.

To others, Jesus was a miracle worker. To others, Jesus was a master teacher. To others, Jesus was the hope of Israel. But to John, he was all of these and more. To John, Jesus was a friend.

You don't abandon a friend—not even when that friend is dead. John stayed close to Jesus.

He had a habit of doing this. He was close to Jesus in the Upper Room. He was close to Jesus in the Garden of Gethsemane. He was at the foot of the cross at the crucifixion, and he was a quick walk from the tomb at the burial.

> Did he understand Jesus? No.
>
> Was he glad Jesus did what he did? No.
>
> But did he leave Jesus? No.

HE CHOSE THE NAILS

We forget that

IMPOSSIBLE

is one of God's favorite words.

Mary Magdalene at Jesus' Tomb

A party was the last thing Mary Magdalene expected as she approached the tomb on that Sunday morning. The last few days had brought nothing to celebrate. The Jews could celebrate—Jesus was out of the way. The soldiers could celebrate— their work was done. But Mary couldn't celebrate. To her the last few days had brought nothing but tragedy.

MARY HAD BEEN THERE. She had heard the leaders clamor for Jesus' blood. She had witnessed the Roman whip rip the skin off his back. She had winced as the thorns sliced his brow and wept at the weight of the cross.

In the Louvre there is a painting of the scene of the cross. In the painting the stars are dead and the world is wrapped in darkness. In the shadows there is a kneeling form. It is Mary. She is holding her hands and lips against the bleeding feet of the Christ.

We don't know if Mary did that, but we know she could have. She was there. She was there to hold her arm around the shoulder of Mary the mother of Jesus. She was there to close his eyes. She was there.

So it's not surprising that she wants to be there again.

In the early morning mist she arises from her mat, takes her spices and aloes, and leaves her house, past the Gate of Gennath and up to the hillside. She anticipates a somber task. By now the body will be swollen. His face will be white. Death's odor will be pungent.

A gray sky gives way to gold as she walks up the narrow trail. As she rounds the final bend, she gasps. The rock in front of the grave is pushed back.

"Someone took the body." She runs to awaken Peter and John. They rush to see for themselves. She tries to keep up with them but can't.

Peter comes out of the tomb bewildered and John comes out believing, but Mary just sits in front of it weeping. The two men go home and leave her alone with her grief.

But something tells her she is not alone. Maybe she hears a noise. Maybe she hears a whisper. Or maybe she just hears her own heart tell her to take a look for herself.

Whatever the reason, she does. She stoops down, sticks her head into the hewn entrance, and waits for her eyes to adjust to the dark.

"Why are you crying?" She sees what looks to be a man, but he's white—radiantly white. He is one of two lights on either end of the vacant slab. Two candles blazing on an altar.

"Why are you crying?" An uncommon question to be asked in a cemetery. In fact, the question is rude. That is, unless the questioner knows something the questionee doesn't.

"They have taken my Lord away, and I don't know where they have put him."

She still calls him "my Lord." As far as she knows, his lips were silent. As far as she knows, his corpse had been carted off by grave robbers. But in spite of it all, he is still her Lord.

Such devotion moves Jesus. It moves him closer to her. So close she hears him breathing. She turns and there he stands. She thinks he is the gardener.

Now, Jesus could have revealed himself at this point. He could have called for an angel to present him or a band to announce his presence. But he didn't.

"Why are you crying? Who is it you are looking for?" (John 20:1–18 NIV).

He doesn't leave her wondering long, just long enough to remind us that he loves to surprise us. He waits for us to despair of human strength and then intervenes with heavenly. God waits for us to give up and then—surprise!

And listen to the surprise as Mary's name is spoken by a man she loved—a man she had buried.

"Miriam."

God appearing at the strangest of places. Doing the strangest of things. Stretching smiles where there had hung only frowns. Placing twinkles where there were only tears. Hanging a bright star in a dark sky. Arching rainbows in the midst of thunderclouds. Calling names in a cemetery.

"Miriam," he said softly, "surprise!"

Mary was shocked. It's not often you hear your name spoken by an eternal tongue. But when she did, she recognized it. And when she did, she responded correctly. She worshiped him.

Six Hours One Friday

WHO IS IT
YOU ARE LOOKING FOR?

Jesus

His Resurrected Body

Jesus appeared to the followers in a flesh-and-bone body: "A spirit does not have flesh and bones as you see that I have" (Luke 24:39 NASB). His resurrected body was a real body, real enough to walk on the road to Emmaus, to be mistaken for that of a gardener, to swallow fish at breakfast. ✳ In the same breath, Jesus' real body was really different. The Emmaus disciples didn't recognize him, and walls didn't stop him. Mark tried to describe the new look and settled for "[Jesus] appeared in another form" (Mark 16:12 NKJV). While his body was the same, it was better; it was glorified. It was a heavenly body. ✳ And I can't find the passage that says he shed it. He ascended in it. "He was lifted up while they were looking on, and a cloud received Him out of their sight" (Acts 1:9 NASB). He will return in it. The angel told the followers, "This Jesus, who has been taken up from you into heaven, will come in just the same way as you have watched Him go into heaven" (Acts 1:11 NASB). ✳ The God-man is still both. The hands that blessed the bread of the boy now bless the prayers of the millions. And the mouth that commissions angels is the mouth that kissed children. ✳ You know what this means? The greatest force in the cosmos understands and intercedes for you. "We have an Advocate with the Father, Jesus Christ the righteous" (1 John 2:1 NASB).

NEXT DOOR SAVIOR

HE LOVES WITH AN

unfailing love.

Peter's Breakfast with Jesus

SEE THE FELLOW in the shadows? That's Peter. Peter the apostle. Peter the impetuous. Peter the passionate. He once walked on water. Stepped right out of the boat onto the lake. He'll soon preach to thousands. Fearless before friends and foes alike. But tonight the one who stepped on the water has hurried into hiding. The one who will speak with power is weeping in pain.

Not sniffling or whimpering, but weeping. Bawling. Bearded face buried in thick hands. His howl echoing in the Jerusalem night. What hurts more? The fact that he did it? Or the fact that he swore he never would?

"Lord, I am ready to go with you to prison and even to die with you!" he pledged only hours earlier. "But Jesus said, 'Peter, before the rooster crows this day, you will say three times that you don't know me'" (Luke 22:33–34 NCV).

Denying Christ on the night of his betrayal was bad enough, but did he have to boast that he wouldn't? And one denial was pitiful, but three? Three denials were horrific, but did he have to curse? "Peter began to place a curse on himself and swear, 'I don't know the man'" (Matthew 26:74 NCV).

And now, awash in a whirlpool of sorrow, Peter is hiding. Peter is weeping. And soon Peter will be fishing.

We wonder why he goes fishing. We know why he goes to Galilee. He had been told that the risen Christ would meet the disciples there. The arranged meeting place is not the sea, however, but a mountain (Matthew 28:16). If the followers were to meet Jesus on a mountain, what are they doing in a boat? No one told them to fish, but that's what they did. "Simon Peter said, 'I am going out to fish.' The others said, 'We will go with you'" (John 21:3 NCV). Besides, didn't Peter quit fishing? Two years earlier, when Jesus called him to fish for men, didn't he drop his net and follow? We haven't seen him fish since. We never see him fish again. Why is he fishing now? Especially now! Jesus has risen from the dead. Peter has seen the empty tomb. Who could fish at a time like this?

Were they hungry? Perhaps that's the sum of it. Maybe the expedition was born out of growling stomachs.

Or then again, maybe it was born out of a broken heart.

You see, Peter could not deny his denial. The empty tomb did not erase the crowing rooster. Christ had returned, but Peter wondered, he must have wondered, "After what I did, would he return for someone like me?"

We've wondered the same. Is Peter the only person to do the very thing he swore he'd never do?

"Infidelity is behind me!"

"From now on, I'm going to bridle my tongue."

"No more shady deals. I've learned my lesson."

Oh, the volume of our boasting. And, oh, the heartbreak of our shame.

Rather than resist the flirting, we return it.

Rather than ignore the gossip, we share it.

Rather than stick to the truth, we shade it.

And the rooster crows, and conviction pierces, and Peter has a partner in the shadows. We weep as Peter wept, and we do what Peter did. We go fishing. We go back to our old lives. We return to our pre-Jesus practices. We do what comes naturally, rather than what comes spiritually. And we question whether Jesus has a place for folks like us.

Jesus answers that question. He answers it for you and me and all who tend to "Peter out" on Christ. His answer came on the shore of the sea in a gift to Peter. You know what Jesus did? Split the waters? Turn the boat to gold and the nets to silver? No, Jesus did something much more meaningful. He invited Peter to breakfast. Jesus prepared a meal.

Of course, the breakfast was one special moment among several that morning. There was the great catch of fish and the recognition of Jesus. The plunge of Peter and the paddling of the disciples. And there was the moment they reached the shore and found Jesus next to a fire of coals. The fish were sizzling, and the bread was waiting, and the defeater of hell and the ruler of heaven invited his friends to sit down and have a bite to eat.

No one could have been more grateful than Peter.

TRAVELING LIGHT

The idea that a virgin would be selected by God to bear himself. . . . The notion that God would don a scalp and toes and two eyes. . . . The thought that the King of the universe would sneeze and burp and get bit by mosquitoes. . . .
It's too incredible. Too revolutionary.
We would never create such a Savior.
We aren't that daring. . . .

In our wildest imaginings we wouldn't conjure
a king who becomes one of us.

But God did. God did what we wouldn't dare dream.
He did what we couldn't imagine.
He became a man so we could trust him.
He became a sacrifice so we could know him.
And he defeated death so we could follow him.

AND THE ANGELS WERE SILENT

HIS LEGACY

Jesus...

those who saw him
were never the same.

Christ came to earth for one reason:

to give his life as a ransom for you,

for me,

FOR ALL OF US.

HE SACRIFICED HIMSELF
TO GIVE US
A SECOND CHANCE.

He Did It Just for You

WHEN GOD ENTERED TIME and became a man, he who was boundless became bound. Imprisoned in flesh. Restricted by weary-prone muscles and eyelids. For more than three decades, his once limitless reach would be limited to the stretch of an arm, his speed checked to the pace of human feet.

I wonder, was he ever tempted to reclaim his boundlessness? In the middle of a long trip, did he ever consider transporting himself to the next city? When the rain chilled his bones, was he tempted to change the weather? When the heat parched his lips, did he give thought to popping over to the Caribbean for some refreshment?

If ever he entertained such thoughts, he never gave in to them. Not once. Stop and think about this. Not once did Christ use his supernatural powers for personal comfort. With one word he could've transformed the hard earth into a soft bed, but he didn't. With a wave of his hand, he could've boomeranged the spit of his accusers back into their faces, but he didn't. With an arch of his brow, he could've paralyzed the hand of the soldier as he braided the crown of thorns. But he didn't.

Want to know the coolest thing about the coming?

Not that the One who played marbles with the stars gave it up to play marbles with marbles. Or that the One who hung the galaxies gave it up to hang doorjambs to the displeasure of a cranky client who wanted everything yesterday but couldn't pay for anything until tomorrow.

Not that he, in an instant, went from needing nothing to needing air, food, a tub of hot water and salts for his tired feet, and, more than anything, needing somebody—anybody—who was more concerned about where he would spend eternity than where he would spend Friday's paycheck.

Or that he resisted the urge to fry the two-bit, self-appointed hall monitors of holiness who dared suggest that he was doing the work of the devil.

Not that he kept his cool while the dozen best friends he ever had felt the heat and got out of the kitchen. Or that he gave no command to the angels who begged, "Just give the nod, Lord. One word and these demons will be deviled eggs."

Not that he refused to defend himself when blamed for every sin of every slut and sailor since Adam. Or that he stood silent as a million guilty verdicts echoed in the tribunal of heaven and the giver of light was left in the chill of a sinner's night.

Not even that after three days in a dark hole he stepped into the Easter sunrise with a smile and a swagger and a question for lowly Lucifer—"Is that your best punch?"

That was cool, incredibly cool.

But want to know the coolest thing about the One who gave up the crown of heaven for a crown of thorns?

He did it for you. *Just for you.*

Jesus says

HE IS THE SOLUTION

for weariness of soul.

His Goodness and Mercy

Dare we envision a God who follows us? Who follows us with "goodness and mercy" all the days of our lives? ❃ The disciples of Jesus knew the feeling of being followed by God. They were rain soaked and shivering when they looked over their shoulders and saw Jesus walking toward them. God had followed them into the storm. ❃ An unnamed Samaritan woman knew the same. She was alone in life and alone at the well when she looked over her shoulder and heard a Messiah speaking. God had followed her through her pain. ❃ John the Apostle was banished on Patmos when he looked over his shoulder and saw the skies begin to open. God had followed him into his exile. ❃ Lazarus was three days dead in a sealed tomb when he heard a voice, lifted his head, and looked over his shoulder and saw Jesus standing. God had followed him into death. ❃ Peter had denied his Lord and gone back to fishing when he heard his name and looked over his shoulder and saw Jesus cooking breakfast. God had followed him in spite of his failure. ❃ God is the God who follows. I wonder . . . have you sensed him following you? Still he follows. Never forcing us. Never leaving us. Patiently persistent. Faithfully present. Using all of his power to convince us that he is who he is and that he can be trusted to lead us home. ❃ His goodness and mercy will follow us all the days of our lives.

Traveling Light

The belief of French philosopher Voltaire: The Bible and Christianity would pass within a hundred years. He died in 1778; the movement continues.

The pronouncement of Friedrich Nietzsche in 1882: "God is dead." The dawn of science, he believed, would be the doom of faith. Science has dawned; the movement continues.

The way a Communist dictionary defined the Bible: "It is a collection of fantastic legends without any scientific support." Communism is diminishing; the movement continues.

THE DISCOVERY made by every person who has tried to bury the faith. The same as the one made by those who tried to bury its Founder: He won't stay in the tomb.

The facts. The movement has never been stronger. Over one billion Catholics and nearly as many Protestants.

The question. How do we explain it? Jesus was a backwater peasant. He never wrote a book, never held an office. He never journeyed more than two hundred miles from his hometown. Friends left him. One betrayed him. Those he helped forgot him. Prior to his death they abandoned him. But after his death they couldn't resist him. What made the difference?

The answer. His death and resurrection. For when he died, so did your sin. And when he rose, so did your hope. For when he rose, your grave was changed from a final residence to temporary housing.

The reason he did it. The face in your mirror.

The verdict after two millenniums. Herod was right: There is room for only one King.

HE CHOSE THE NAILS

He Is Love

"Love . . . endures all things" (1 Corinthians 13:4–7 NASB).

He could have given up. No one would have known otherwise. Jesus could have given up.

One look at the womb could have discouraged him. God is as unbridled as the air and limitless as the sky. Would he reduce his world to the belly of a girl for nine months?

And nine months? There is another reason to quit. Heaven has no months. Heaven has no time. Or, perhaps better said, heaven has all the time. It's we who are running out. Ours passes so quickly that we measure it by the second. Wouldn't Christ rather stay on the other side of the ridge of time?

He could have. He could have given up. If not, at least he could have stopped short. Did he have to become flesh? How about becoming light? Here is an idea. Heaven could open, and Christ could fall on the earth in the form of a white light. And then in the light there could be a voice, a booming, thundering, teeth-shaking voice. Toss in a gust of wind and the angels for background vocals, and the whole world notices!

As things turned out, when he came, hardly anyone noticed. Bethlehem held no parade. The village offered no banquet. You'd think a holiday would have been appropriate. At least a few streamers for the stable.

And the stable. Is that not yet another reason for Christ to back out? Stables are smelly, dirty. Stables have no linoleum floors or oxygen tanks. How are they going to cut the umbilical cord? And who is going to cut the umbilical cord? Joseph? A small-time carpenter from a one-camel town? Is there not a better father for God? Someone with an education, a pedigree? Someone with a bit of clout? This fellow couldn't even swing a room at the hotel. You think he's got what it takes to be the father to the Maker of the universe?

Jesus could have given up. Imagine the change he had to make, the distance he had to travel. What would it be like to become flesh? . . .

Love goes the distance . . . and Christ traveled from limitless eternity to be confined by time in order to become one of us. He didn't have to. He could have given up. At any step along the way he could have called it quits.

When he saw the size of the womb, he could have stopped.

When he saw how tiny his hand would be, how soft his voice would be, how hungry his tummy would be, he could have stopped. At the first whiff of the stinky stable, at the first gust of cold air. The first time he scraped his knee or blew his nose or tasted burnt bagels, he could have turned and walked out.

When he saw the dirt floor of his Nazareth house. When Joseph gave him a chore to do. When his fellow students were dozing off during the reading of the Torah, his Torah. When the neighbor took his name in vain. When the lazy farmer blamed his poor crop on God. At any point Jesus could have said, "That's it! That's enough! I'm going home." But he didn't.

He didn't, because he is love. And "love . . . endures all things" (1 Corinthians 13:4–7 NKJV).

A LOVE WORTH GIVING

Jesus

LOVE GOES THE DISTANCE

HE WAS GOD-MAN.

Jesus was not a godlike man, nor a manlike God.
He was God-man.

Midwifed by a carpenter.

Bathed by a peasant girl.

The maker of the world with a bellybutton.

The author of the Torah being taught the Torah.

Heaven's human. And because he was, we are left with
scratch-your-head, double-blink,
what's-wrong-with-this-picture? moments like these:

Bordeaux instead of H_2O.

A cripple sponsoring the town dance.

A sack lunch satisfying five thousand tummies.

And, most of all, a grave: guarded by soldiers,
sealed by a rock, yet vacated by a three-days-dead man.

What do we do with such moments?

What do we do with such a person? We applaud men for
doing good things. We enshrine God for doing great things.
But when a man does God things?

One thing is certain, we can't ignore him.

NEXT DOOR SAVIOR

HE INVITES US TO LOVE HIM.

HE URGES US TO LOVE HIM.

But, in the end, the choice is yours and mine.

HIS NAME IS

Jesus

JESUS SAID, "COME FOLLOW ME, AND I WILL MAKE YOU FISH FOR PEOPLE."

MATTHEW 4:19 NCV

Jesus said, "I am with you for only a short time, and then I go to the one who sent me."

THEN JESUS CAME TO THEM AND SAID, "ALL
AUTHORITY IN HEAVEN AND ON EARTH HAS
BEEN GIVEN TO ME."

MATTHEW 28:18 **NIV**

Jesus said to her,

"I AM THE RESURRECTION AND THE LIFE.

The one who believes in me

   will live, even though they die."

JOHN 11:25 NIV

SOURCES

All of the material in this book was originally published in the following books by Max Lucado.

All copyrights to the original works are held by the author, Max Lucado.

He Still Moves Stones (Nashville: Thomas Nelson, Inc., 1993).
A Gentle Thunder (Nashville: Thomas Nelson, Inc., 1995).
Just Like Jesus (Nashville: Thomas Nelson, Inc., 1998).
When Christ Comes (Nashville: Thomas Nelson, Inc., 1999).
Traveling Light (Nashville: Thomas Nelson, Inc., 2000).
He Chose the Nails (Nashville: Thomas Nelson, Inc., 2000).
A Love Worth Giving (Nashville: Thomas Nelson, Inc., 2002).
And the Angels Were Silent (Nashville: Thomas Nelson, Inc., 2003).
Next Door Savior (Nashville: Thomas Nelson, Inc., 2003).
No Wonder They Call Him the Savior (Nashville: Thomas Nelson, Inc., 2003).
Six Hours One Friday (Nashville: Thomas Nelson, Inc., 2003).
Come Thirsty (Nashville: Thomas Nelson, Inc., 2004).
It's Not About Me (Nashville: Thomas Nelson, Inc., 2004).
Every Day Deserves a Chance (Nashville: Thomas Nelson, Inc., 2007).